Moving

BY FRED ROGERS

photographs by Jim Judkis

G. P. PUTNAM'S SONS
New York

With special thanks to: Nan Earl Newell,
Margaret B. McFarland, Ph.D., Senior Consultant;
Barry N. Head; the Smith family; Joe Gardner
and the other parents and children who agreed
to help us with the book.

Printed in the United States of America
Project Director: Margy Whitmer
Book design by Kathleen Westray
Library of Congress Cataloging-in-Publication Data
Rogers, Fred.   Moving.
(A Mister Rogers' First experience book)
Summary: Describes in detail the process
of moving, as well as the irritation and
uncertainty, the sorrow and the excitement.
1. Moving, Household—Juvenile literature.   [1. Moving,
Household]   I. Judkis, Jim, ill.   II. Title.   III. Series:
Rogers, Fred.   Mister Rogers' First experience book.
TX307.R64   1987   648'.9   86-9426
ISBN 0-399-21383-X
ISBN 0-399-21384-8 (pbk.)
First impression

For a family with young children, moving to a new home can be an especially stressful time. Adults and children alike often find it hard to say goodbye to the people and places they know and love. Very young children who have not yet made close attachments outside the family may be worried most by the moving around of familiar objects and the upsets in familiar routines. We need to help them realize that indeed they and their belongings will be going to the new home, that they will be taken care of.

The weeks leading up to moving day are often hectic and busy. Finding ways to include young children in some of the moving process can help them understand that they're a real part of what's going on. You might give them a special box to pack their own way—a box they can unpack in the new home. That could give them a sense of continuity and a feeling that they still have some control in an otherwise unsettled time. And encouraging them to talk about their feelings can help them experience a move as the adventure that it truly can be.

—Fred Rogers

It's a good feeling to know the neighborhood where you live
and to know some of the people who live there . . .

. . . but families don't always live in the same place forever.

Some families move because the mother or father has a new job somewhere else. Other families move because they need a new place to live that's larger or smaller. Whatever the reasons are for the move, it's important to remember that children are part of the family, and they go along, too.

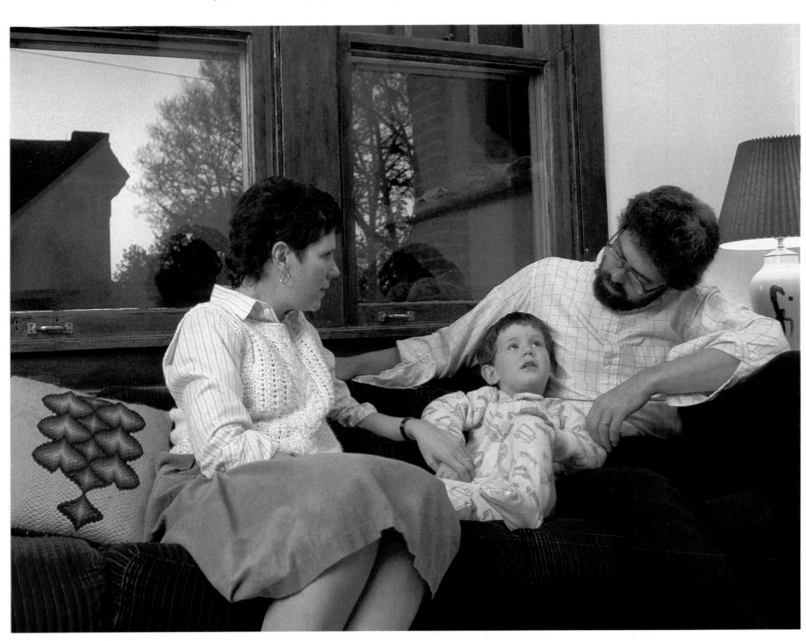

It can be exciting to think about moving to a new place. But grownups *and* children can feel sad about saying goodbye to the people and places they've come to know and love. Sometimes it's hard to be sure just *how* you feel about moving.

When it's time to move, there's so much to do! People have to decide what to take to their new home and what to leave behind. They might sell or give away things that the new home already has, or things that they just don't need or want anymore. But they almost always leave things like bathtubs and sinks or toilets—most of those things can't be moved.

Children often wonder about what will go and what will stay. It can help to tell the grownups you love what *you're* wondering about and what you're feeling.

People can get cranky when they're getting ready to move. Nothing seems to be in its right place anymore. It can be hard to fix a meal, or to play, when things are getting packed away. It can be hard to find a quiet time, just for you, with someone you love . . .

. . . but there can be times for hugs.

Many of the things that are going to go along are packed carefully in suitcases and boxes—clothes that don't need to be worn right away, books, toys, small things, and breakable things like dishes and lamps. All these things will travel to your new home.

You might want to ask your mom or dad to let you pack some of your own things. Are there a few things you'd rather *not* pack so that you can play with them on the trip to your new home?

Families sometimes use cars or small trucks to move things. Friends and neighbors often help.

When families have to move a lot of big things, they get a truck called a *moving van*. The people who come with the moving van know how to help families move. That's why they're called "movers." Movers also know that moving can be a hard time for a family.

Movers carry the boxes and furniture out of the old
house and put them into the van.

They don't put people or pets into the van—and, of course, houses would be too big to go into the van—but they do put the things in that will go to your new home.

A moving van can seem very big—and maybe even a little scary at first—but it has to be very big so that it can carry lots of things.

If you wonder what the inside of the van looks like, you could ask your movers to show you. They might even let you carry something into the van.

When the van gets to the new house, the movers will take everything out and help to put the big things where they belong.

Unpacking takes time. You may
be able to help decide where your
bed and clothes and books and
toys will go in your new room.

A new house can look very empty and strange until you fill it with the things that make it look like your home.

Of course, what makes it feel *most* like your home is the people you love being there.

There's lots to discover in a new place! There are new streets, new schools, and of course, new places to play. There are new people to meet and new friends to make. It can help to know that children don't have to get used to all these new things by themselves.

In every neighborhood there are grownups who like children and want to help them. These grownups know that people can't get used to new things all at once and that they need to take their time.

You might miss your old friends and wish that they could have come with you. But you can keep in touch with them by writing letters, or sending them pictures or drawings,

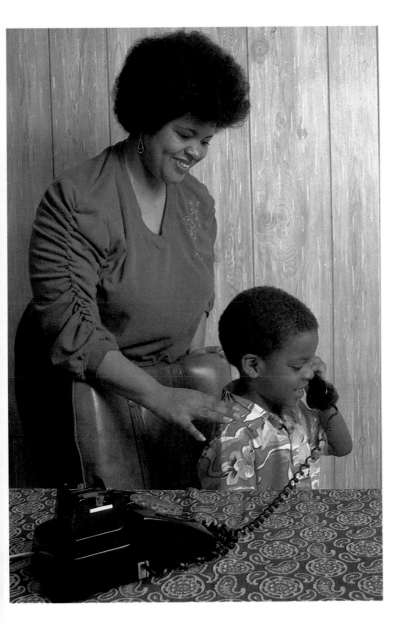

by talking to them on the telephone, or sometimes, by making plans to visit. There may be lots you'll want to tell them about the new things you're seeing and doing.

When you think about your old house, you can know
that it's still there. And when you remember your old
friends, you can know that they are still your friends,
even after you move.

Wherever you are, you're still the same person —the same person your old friends will be remembering.

There are times when everyone in the whole world has to say goodbye to places and friends they love. That's hard. But when you can do that, and say hello to *new* friends and *new* places, the people who love you best can be really proud of the way you're growing. And it can be such a good feeling for you, too!